Children and Modern AI

Challenges and Opportunities

Editorial Director: Dr. M. K. Pour
Editor: Meaghan Austin
Illustrator and Graphic Designer: Phil Shickler

Published in the United States of America by
e-Robotic Press (an imprint of IGI Global Scientific Publishing)
250 Broadway, Suite 620
New York, NY 10007
Tel: 646-551-4700
Email: customerservice@e-roboticpress.com
Website: www.e-roboticpress.com

ISBN: 978-1-971794-64-8

Dear Readers,

In today's rapidly evolving age of artificial intelligence (AI), many children are hearing about and discussing AI without truly understanding what it is or how it works. At the same time, many parents are wondering whether their children are learning enough about AI and its far-reaching impact on their lives. In other words: *Are we preparing our children for the challenges AI presents today—and the even greater challenges it will bring in the future?*

The primary goal of *Children and Modern AI: Challenges and Opportunities* is to educate children and spark their curiosity by exploring AI's history, core concepts, real-world applications, research, careers, and the many opportunities AI systems offer.

As a former technology professor at a major state university for more than 20 years—and now as a parent of two children, ages 9 and 6—my wife and I face the same challenge as many other parents: preparing our children to navigate a world increasingly shaped by AI. It is essential to recognize that the only way our children can truly benefit from AI technologies is by developing their own intellectual and analytical abilities. AI tools are, ultimately, just that—tools created by humans to enhance productivity and improve our lives.

As parents, we must remain mindful that if we do not encourage our children to strengthen their minds, they may struggle to keep up with these systems. We certainly don't want them to become dependent on AI or allow it to think on their behalf. Encourage your children to use their own brains—to solve problems, generate ideas, and think critically—rather than relying entirely on AI to do the thinking for them.

These challenges are real, and they are not easy. But we have no alternative. We want our children to create, control, and master AI systems—not to be controlled by them.

Remember: knowledge is power!

Sincerely,

Dr. M. K. Pour

Table of Contents

Introduction to the World of AI 4

Historical Perspectives of AI 6

What Is AI? 9

What are the Different Kinds of AI? 12

Current Major Applications of AI 15

Future Applications of AI 18

Problems and Limitations of AI 21

Ethical and Social Responsibility of Using AI 24

Future Possibilities in an AI World 27

Additional Resources to Learn More About AI 29

Bibliography 30

Introduction to the World of AI

For thousands of years, people have invented tools to make life easier. Over time, simple tools turned into machines, and machines led to computers. Today, computers can do more than follow basic instructions. The newest step in this story is artificial intelligence, or AI.

AI helps computers do tasks that seem smart. Instead of using only strict, step-by-step rules, many AI systems learn from information, also called data. AI can look at pictures, words, numbers, and sounds. Then it finds patterns and uses them to make the best guess or choice. This is a bit like how people learn from practice and experience.

AI is already part of everyday life, even when you do not notice it. It can answer questions online, suggest videos and games, and power voice assistants.

Introduction to the World of AI

AI is also used in medicine to study health information and in science to support research. In schools, AI tools can help students practice skills and help teachers plan lessons.

AI can manage large amounts of information and do certain tasks quickly. This can save time and make learning more efficient. But AI is not perfect. It can make mistakes or give confusing answers, so people still need to check its work and make the final decision.

In this book, you will learn what AI is and how it works. You will also learn about different kinds of AI and how people use AI today. We will also look at challenges, like mistakes and unfair results, and why responsible use matters. AI can support people and boost creativity, but it should not replace human thinking. Before we explore how modern AI works, we will first look at how AI developed over time.

Historical Perspective of AI

Long before modern computers, people imagined automata. These were machines that could move and act on their own. Old stories show that people have been curious for a long time about building lifelike machines.

Over time, these ideas turned into real inventions. Engineers in places like Greece, China, and the Arabian and Persian worlds built early machines that could move, make sounds, and follow simple instructions. In ancient China, people used water-powered figures for education and entertainment. These machines helped people see how motion and energy work together.

Historical Perspective of AI

In the 1950s, scientists began to think of and study AI more seriously. Alan Turing, a British mathematician and computer scientist, asked an important question: Can machines think? Early AI programs were limited. They followed strict, rule-based instructions. As computers got faster and stronger, AI programs improved and could solve harder problems.

At first, AI could do only specific tasks. It could not learn, adjust to new situations, or handle complex problems. As computer technology improved, researchers created programs that could work with more information and make better predictions.

Historical Perspective of AI

By the late 1900s and early 2000s, AI research grew quickly. Better computer power, more data storage, and machine learning helped AI find patterns, understand language, and make predictions. Today, AI is used in many fields, including education, medicine, transportation, and scientific research.

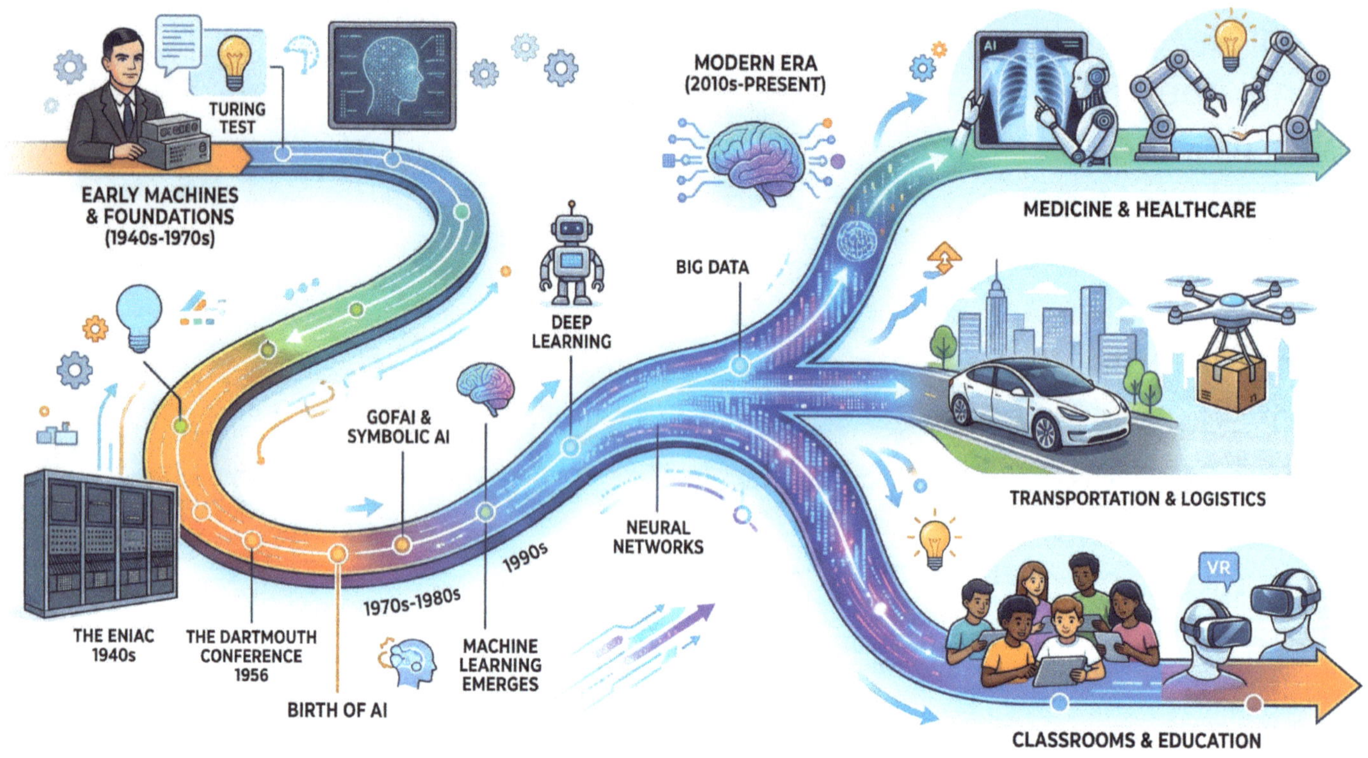

Modern AI can improve over time by learning from results and fixing mistakes. It can compare what worked and what did not. Then it updates how it makes choices. This shows how AI has grown from a big idea into practical tools. These tools can support human work and decision-making, and they work best when people stay involved.

What Is AI?

AI stands for Artificial Intelligence. It is technology that helps computers do tasks that seem intelligent. For example, AI can learn from information, find patterns, make decisions, and solve problems. AI is not one single machine or app. It is a set of tools that work together, including data, math, and computer programs. These tools help a computer make a prediction or decide what to do next.

AI learns by finding patterns in data. People learn patterns in a similar way. For example, you learn what a cat looks like by seeing many cats over time. You notice features like whiskers, pointed ears, and a tail. After getting enough practice, you can spot a cat even if you have never seen that exact one before. AI can learn the same way by studying many examples, such as thousands of cat pictures.

What Is AI?

Data is the foundation of AI learning. Data is information such as pictures, words, numbers, sounds, and videos. Every day, data is created by photos, messages, music, websites, sensors, and weather reports. Data quality matters. Just as students learn better from accurate books, AI learns better from high-quality data. If the data is incorrect, incomplete, or biased, the AI's results can also be incorrect or unfair.

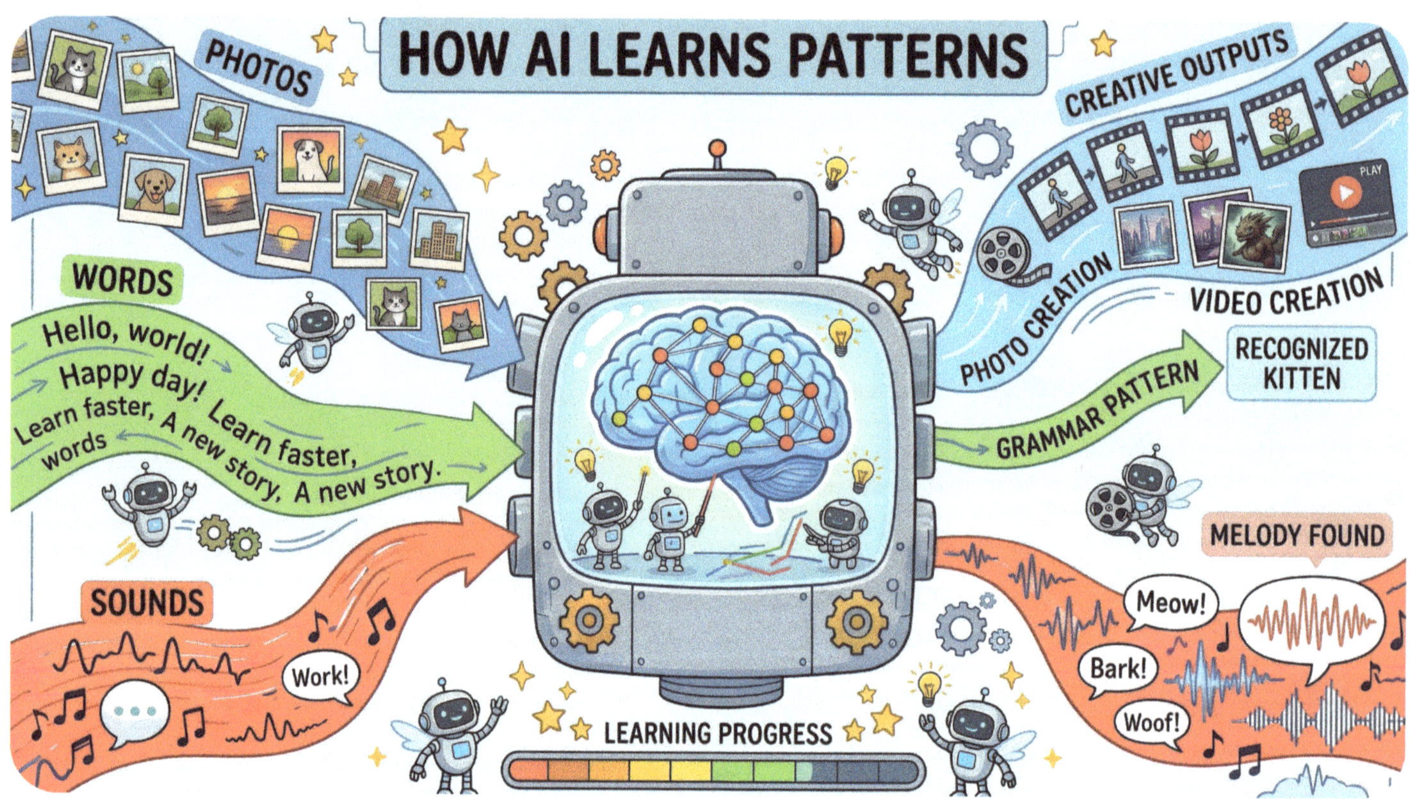

AI relies on algorithms to learn and make decisions. An algorithm is a step-by-step set of rules a computer follows to solve a problem. Different AI systems use different algorithms depending on the task. Some help AI systems understand language, while others help it recognize images or make predictions. AI does not understand like a human. It finds patterns that often lead to certain results.

What Is AI?

One common way AI learns is machine learning (when a computer learns from examples instead of being programmed for every step). A more advanced type is deep learning (machine learning that uses many layers of pattern-finding). Deep learning uses neural networks, which are computer models inspired by the human brain. Neural networks use layers that process information step by step. Deep learning often needs powerful computers, lots of data, and a lot of energy.

Even with these advances, AI does not think like humans. It does not have emotions, common sense, or personal experiences. AI makes predictions based on patterns, so it can still make mistakes, especially in new situations. That is why people must stay involved. For important choices, humans should review AI results and decide what to do.

What Are the Different Kinds of AI?

Not all AI works the same way. Each AI system is built for a purpose. Some AI analyzes information to sort it, organize it, or make predictions. For example, it might help forecast weather, recommend products, or spot trends in a large dataset. Other AI creates new content, such as writing stories, generating images, composing music, or designing artwork. Each type can be useful because it solves different kinds of problems.

TWO FACETS OF ARTIFICIAL INTELLIGENCE

What Are the Different Kinds of AI?

AI can also be grouped by how many tasks it can do. Most AI used today is called narrow AI. Narrow AI does one specific job well, such as recognizing faces, translating languages, or recommending videos. Scientists also talk about general AI. General AI would be able to learn and reason across many kinds of tasks like a human. General AI is still an idea and does not exist yet.

Another way to group AI is by how it learns from information. In supervised learning, the AI trains on examples that include the correct answers. In unsupervised learning, the AI looks at data and tries to find patterns without being told the answers. In reinforcement learning, the AI learns by trying actions, getting feedback, and improving through trial and error.

What Are the Different Kinds of AI?

Some deep learning systems focus on language. One important example is a Large Language Model (LLM), which is an AI system trained using huge amounts of text. LLMs can generate responses using words. They can answer questions, explain ideas, summarize information, and help with writing.

Current Major Applications of AI

AI helps people every day in many parts of life. Even when you do not notice it, AI can work in the background to make tasks easier, faster, and more accurate. It can help answer questions, recommend content, improve communication, support learning, and assist with decision-making. Here are some examples of how AI is used today:

- AI can help build a working website with useful features in just a few hours.
- In the retail industry, AI helps with simple, time-consuming tasks such as managing product inventory. This helps businesses avoid overstocking or running out of products.
- Modern rail systems use AI to analyze data from sensors on tracks and trains. This helps spot tiny cracks and loose rails. AI can find problems days or weeks earlier than traditional inspections.

Current Major Applications of AI

- Some earbuds today use AI to translate foreign languages in real-time. They can listen to someone speaking and quickly turn the speech into the user's native language.
- AI spam filters analyze both the meaning of emails and how people handle their messages to keep unwanted emails out of the inbox.
- Some flowerpots use AI to water plants automatically by tracking light, humidity, and temperature.
- AI can recognize people in photographs faster than a human can, even if the picture is blurry or dark.
- AI helps scientists study endangered animals without disturbing them by using special cameras. These cameras can recognize different species and even individual animals by patterns like stripes or spots.

Current Major Applications of AI

- AI helps architects design better buildings by testing lots of ideas on a computer before anything is actually built.
- AI-powered eye-tracking technology helps people with physical disabilities use computers. It follows where they look and turns their eye movements into actions on the screen.
- Some banks use AI to watch how money is spent. These smart systems learn what normal spending looks like and look for strange activity. If something unusual happens, the bank can check to see if it is fraud.
- Some police departments use AI to review large amounts of crime data and spot unusual patterns. This can help them decide where to focus safety efforts.
- Some AI tools help find learning problems like dyslexia. They can also give students special help and activities to make learning easier.

Future Applications of AI

AI will likely become even more important at school and at work. In many jobs, AI may help with routine tasks like scheduling meetings, answering customer questions, sorting paperwork, and organizing information. When AI handles repetitive work, people can spend more time on creative thinking, problem-solving, and decision-making. Below are some examples of how AI may be used in the future.

- AI companions in nursing homes may help staff by spotting early signs of memory problems, such as dementia or Alzheimer's. They could do this by analyzing changes in a person's voice and facial expressions over time.
- AI may help control traffic lights and suggest better routes. This could reduce traffic jams and help prevent accidents.

Future Applications of AI

- AI tutors may give students extra practice and feedback, and they may track progress over time. They could also help teachers plan more personalized lessons.
- In some restaurants, AI robots may take orders, deliver food, and clear tables. This could help workers focus on customer service and safety.
- AI may help emergency teams respond faster by spotting where help is needed. For example, it could analyze calls, messages, or map data to guide responders.
- Beauty companies may use AI scanners to analyze hair or skin and suggest products. Some systems could even help create custom products that match a customer's needs.
- Governments may use AI and satellite data to predict natural disasters and send warnings sooner. This could help people prepare and stay safe.

Future Applications of AI

- AI-powered underwater robots may explore the deep ocean and help scientists discover new sea life.
- AI may track pollution in real time by studying data from satellites and sensors. This could help scientists understand where pollution is coming from and how it changes.
- AI personal assistants may manage schedules, set reminders, and help people plan their day.
- AI-enabled refrigerators may track what is inside and suggest grocery lists. Some may even place orders, so families do not run out of common items.
- AI may create virtual worlds where students can practice real jobs, such as nursing, engineering, or firefighting. These simulations could help students learn skills in a safe environment.

Problems and Limitations of AI

Limitations and risks are problems or weaknesses with AI. Limitations are things AI cannot do well. Risks are things that could go wrong if people rely on AI too much. Knowing about these issues helps users remember to double-check AI's work and think carefully about its answers. AI is a helpful tool, but it should support human thinking—not replace it.

AI does not think the way humans do. People use feelings, common sense, creativity, and real-life experience when they decide what to do. AI learns by finding patterns in data and following rules. It does not truly understand why something is correct. Because of this, AI can struggle with new or surprising situations. AI can sometimes give incorrect or misleading information. The answer may sound confident, even when it is wrong. This problem is called AI hallucination. For example, an AI tool might make up a book title, a website link, or a "fact" that does not exist. Also, AI answers can be hard to explain because the steps inside the system can be complex.

Problems and Limitations of AI

AI systems depend on good data, strong technology, and other resources. If training data is inaccurate, incomplete, or biased, the AI can give unfair or incorrect results. AI systems can also be expensive to build and run. They may need powerful computers, use a lot of energy, and require regular updates to be useful. These challenges are a reason to use AI thoughtfully.

Problems and Limitations of AI

People can reduce AI risks by using it carefully. Researchers work to make AI more accurate, fair, and easier to understand, but users also matter. For important information, check trusted sources such as books, teachers, experts, or reliable websites. Comparing more than one source and asking, "Does this make sense?" can help prevent mistakes.

Clear rules and teamwork also help. Many schools and workplaces create guidelines for how AI should be used. In important situations, a person should review AI-generated work before a final decision is made. AI works best when people stay involved, ask questions, and use critical thinking.

Ethical and Social Responsibility of Using AI

Ethical and responsible use of AI means using it in kind, fair, and honest ways. Ethics are guidelines about what is right and wrong, and they help people decide how artificial intelligence should be designed and used. AI should never be used to harm others, trick people, invade privacy, or spread false information. Instead, it should be used to help people solve problems and improve daily life in positive and meaningful ways.

THE IMPACT OF TRAINING DATA ON AI BIAS

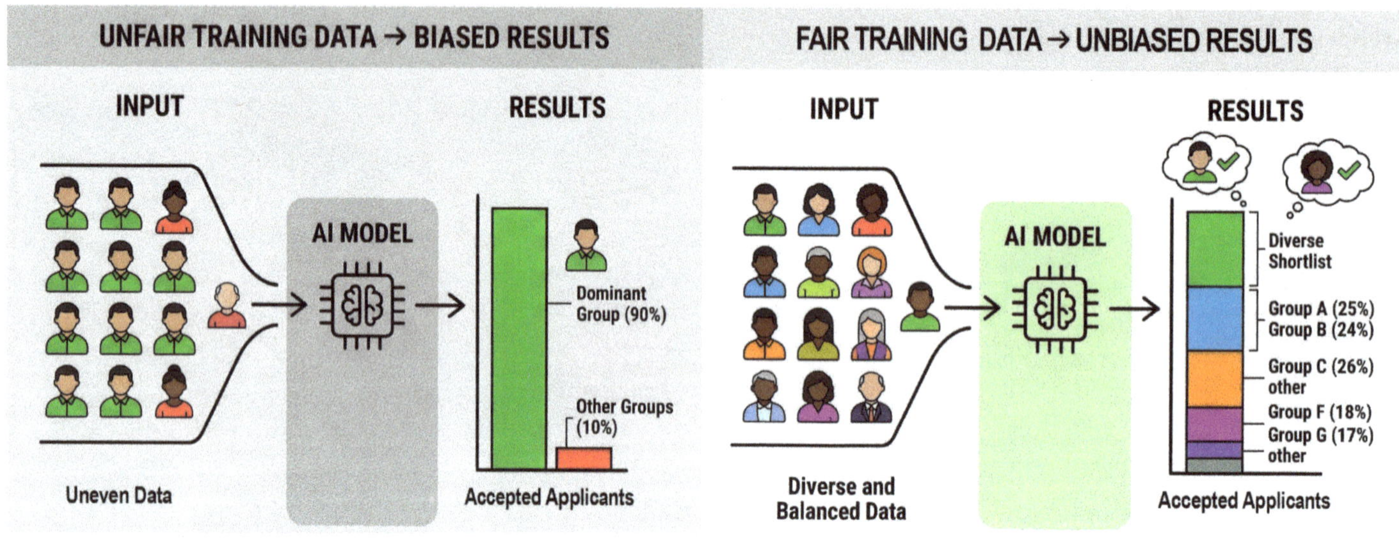

One major ethical concern with AI is bias (when a system is unfair because the data it learned from is unbalanced). For example, if an AI hiring tool is trained on old job data where mostly men were hired, it may incorrectly learn that men should be chosen more often. Another example is facial recognition. If the training data includes mostly lighter-skinned faces, the system may make more mistakes for people with darker skin tones. These examples show why it is important to use diverse, accurate, and representative data when creating AI systems.

Ethical and Social Responsibility of Using AI

Protecting privacy is another important responsibility. Privacy means keeping personal information from being shared or used in ways you did not agree to. AI systems can collect and process data such as voices, locations, photos, videos, or even fingerprints. If this sensitive data is not carefully protected, it could be misused or cause harm. Developers and people who use AI must take steps to keep data secure, limit who can access it, and respect people's right to privacy.

Ethical AI use is especially important in schools. Students should be honest about when and how they use AI tools in their schoolwork. Using AI to copy answers, complete assignments without understanding them, or claim AI-generated work as one's own is still considered cheating. AI should be used as a learning aid—such as helping explain ideas or organize thoughts—not as a replacement for a student's own thinking and effort.

Ethical and Social Responsibility of Using AI

Some simple rules for responsible AI, especially for kids, that are easy to remember:

- **Be safe**: Do not share private or personal information.
- **Be honest**: Do not pretend that AI-generated work is your own.
- **Be kind**: Do not use AI to bully, spread rumors, or harm others.

When people follow these guidelines, AI can be used responsibly and ethically as a helpful tool that supports learning, creativity, and positive decision-making.

Future Possibilities of an AI World

AI is expected to become a normal part of everyday life at home, school, and work. People may use AI on phones and other devices to help with homework, shopping, planning schedules, managing money, and communicating. In schools, AI tools may support personalized learning. In workplaces, AI may help businesses work more efficiently, analyze information faster, and make better-informed decisions. As technology improves, AI tools may become easier to use and more affordable.

As AI becomes more common, some tools may be shared more openly. This is often called open source (when the computer code is shared so others can study it and improve it). When used responsibly, open-source AI can support teamwork and transparency. It can also help more people find and fix problems, which can make AI safer and fairer over time. AI will also help improve other technologies. Computer vision (AI that helps computers "see" and understand images and video) may get better at recognizing objects and actions. Language tools may create better translations and understand meaning and tone. Robotics may become more flexible, so robots can adjust to new places. In homes and cities, smart devices may work together to manage energy, traffic, safety, and services more efficiently.

Future Possibilities of an AI World

In the future, some AI systems may handle different kinds of information at the same time, such as voice, text, and images. This could make AI feel more natural to use. For example, virtual assistants may listen, respond, and help complete online tasks faster. As AI becomes more important, people may create new laws, rules, and ethical guidelines. These can help protect users, prevent misuse, and encourage safe and fair AI.

Additional Resources to Learn More About AI

Below are books and articles you can use to learn more about AI.

- *Co-Intelligence: Living and Working with AI* by Ethan Mollick
- *Artificial Intelligence: A Guide for Thinking Humans* by Melanie Mitchell
- *Human Compatible: Artificial Intelligence and the Problem of Control* by Stuart Russell
- *Artificial General Intelligence: A Revolution Beyond Deep Learning and The Human Brain* by Brent Oster and Gunnar Newquist
- *You Look Like a Thing and I Love You: How Artificial Intelligence Works and Why It's Making the World a Weirder Place* by Janelle Shane
- *Artificial Intelligence Basics: A Non-Technical Introduction* by Tom Taulli
- "Teaching academic writing in the age of AI" by Zara Abrams
- "The Impact of Artificial Intelligence on Modern Society" by Pedro Ramos Brandao
- "Artificial Intelligence and the Future of Teaching and Learning" by the U.S. Department of Education
- "What is an Artificial Intelligence (AI): A Simple Buzzword or a Worthwhile Inevitability?" by Gbadegeshin, et al.
- "A Brief History of Artificial Intelligence: On the Past, Present, and Future of Artificial Intelligence" by Michael Haenlein and Andreas Kaplan
- "An Overview of Artificial Intelligence: Key Concepts and Real-World Applications" by Bhatt, et al.

Bibliography

https://www.history.com/articles/artificial-intelligence-fiction
https://www.theworldofchinese.com/2025/04/history-of-robotic-fantasies-in-ancient-china/
https://robotsauthority.com/the-development-of-early-robots-in-ancient-civilizations/
https://www.ibm.com/think/topics/history-of-artificial-intelligence
https://swisscyberinstitute.com/blog/history-artificial-intelligence/
https://st.llnl.gov/news/look-back/birth-artificial-intelligence-ai-research
https://www.itsprodigy.com/en/news/2025-04-17-artificial-intelligence-why-was-created/
https://theconversation.com/not-everything-we-call-ai-is-actually-artificial-intelligence-heres-what-you-need-to-know-196732
https://www.historytools.org/concepts/early-automata
https://www.coursera.org/articles/history-of-ai?msockid=33d6712d5535611334ca67d1545b6059
https://www.ibm.com/think/topics/artificial-intelligence
https://techpulsion.com/different-types-of-ai/
https://www.britannica.com/science/history-of-artificial-intelligence
https://www.databricks.com/blog/top-ai-use-cases-transforming-industries-2025
https://www.sciencenewstoday.org/how-artificial-intelligence-works-a-beginners-guide
https://www.ibm.com/think/insights/artificial-intelligence-future
https://www.littlelit.ai/post/ai-education-why-kids-must-learn-artificial-intelligence-in-2025
https://www.codiste.com/types-of-ai-models-explained
https://www.codiste.com/types-of-ai-models-explained
https://pecb.com/en/article/artificial-intelligence-ethics-and-social-responsibility
https://spyforkids.com/ai-and-ethics-what-kids-should-know/

www.ingramcontent.com/pod-product-compliance
Lightning Source LLC
LaVergne TN
LVHW060615110826
845154LV00003B/92

* 9 7 8 1 9 7 1 7 9 4 6 4 8 *